THE DEATHWOOD LETTERS

13 Paradise St.
Smelby
31st Jan.

Dear Damian,

I like secrets but I dont get much chance of any because of George always poking his nose in. He did find your letters, but I have now got a realy good hiding place - I hope!

Why dont you and I have a REAL secret, that would show him!! Never mind just writing, we could meet some night when your folks are having one of their boring dinner parties.

Good spellers please note: these letters have been reproduced exactly as written.

THE DEATHWOOD LETTERS

Hazel Townson

RED FOX

For Kenneth again,
with love and thanks

A Red Fox Book

Published by Random Century Children's Books
20 Vauxhall Bridge Road, London SW1V 2SA

A division of the Random Century Group

London Melbourne Sydney Auckland
Johannesburg and agencies throughout the world

First published by Andersen Press Limited 1990

Red Fox edition 1991

Copyright © Hazel Townson 1990

Sketches by Nicholas Flugge

Printed and bound in Great Britain by
Cox & Wyman Ltd, Reading, Berks.

ISBN 0 09 983500 2

Batch the First

13, Paradise Street,
Smelby
28th Dec.

Dear Damian Drake,

I hope you dont mind me writing to you, but I saw your photo in the newspaper and I thought you were ever so brave to climb into that well to rescue your dog Victor. My brother George says you must be mad, risking your neck for a dog, but I think you should get a meddle.

We used to have a dog called Killer, but one night he got lost and we never saw him again. I love dogs. I hope you will write back to me.

I go to St. Simons Middle School. I am in Mr Ramsdens class and he says

I am the best writer.

> *Your admierer,*
> *Frances Bond*

P.S.   I hope this letter reaches you.
Deathwood Hall isn't much of an
address with no road or anything.

DEATHWOOD HALL

Walsea

2nd Jan.

Dear Frances,

I was very pleased to get your letter. Quite a few people wrote to me but you were the only girl. A dog food firm gave me some vouchers and a lady in Portsmouth sent me a book about dogs. I am also going to get a Blue Peter badge. My parents panicked at all the publiscity in case I get kid-naped - (honestly!). I think they were just jellous.

I am sorry you lost your dog Killer. If you like I will send you a big photo of Victor.

I am a pupil at St. Aidan's Academy and am in the Junior 2nd Eleven (in goal).

> Happy New Year!
> Please write again.
> Yours sincerely,
>
> **Damian Drake**

13, Paradise Street,
Smelby
4th Jan.

Dear Damian,

Thank you for writing back to me. I had to laugh though - my brother George thought you were in gaol! He is a rotton speller.

Please do send me the photo of Victor. I will stick it to the wall in my bedroom, next to my drawing of Killer. Killer never had his photo taken be-cause my dad pawned the camera when he lost his job three years ago. My brother George has left school but he hasnt got a job either.

What was it like down the well? You must have been scared. I feel scared if I

*just go down our cellar. I expect you
think thats wet - (wet - get it?) - but
our teacher Mr Ramsden says I have a
vivid imagenation. Why is your place
called Deathwood, has there been a
murder in it or the plage or something? I hope so as this will make it
more interesting.*

*Best wishes from
your freind Frances*

(Call me Frankie, all my freinds do.)

DEATHWOOD HALL

Walsea

7th Jan.

Dear Frankie,

I hope you really don't mind me calling you Frankie as we have not been properly introduced.

Deathwood is pronounced Deethwood like teeth, I don't know of any plagues or murders (yet!) but it was spooky in that WET well. It is an ancient feature of the house and was supposed to be boarded up but I guess it had DRY rot (!) because when Victor jumped on top of it he fell right through. There was an iron ladder going down inside but it was rusty

and some of the rungs were missing.
The smell was awful and it got darker
all the way down. My parents nearly
had a fit when they found out where
I'd been. There's usually somebody
keeping an eye on me (yuck!) so
half the staff got into trouble.

Here is the photo of Victor sitting
on our front lawn. I took it myself, my
camera has a zoom lens. Are you
going to get another dog? If I hadn't
rescued Victor I don't think I would
have wanted another dog.

Can you copy the drawing of Killer
for me?

        All good wishes,
            Your friend, Damian

13 Paradise St.
Smelby
10th Jan.

Dear Damian,

Thank you for the super photo of Victor on your lawn. Your house looks very posh with all those steps curving round and those big stone pots full of flowers. My brother George says a big house like that is sure to be split up into flats. Which flat do you have? I think the top ones are the best, out of everybody's way. My Aunty Nora lives in a flat, but they wont let her keep any pets.

Maybe we'll have another dog if my dad gets a job. We could try the Dogs Home but we'll never get one like

*Killer. I enclose a drawing of Killer,
but its not very good. He was hansomer
than that.*

*Your well sounds worse than our
cellar which is half full of stinky water
most of the time. Once there was a
dead rat floating in it. I never go in
there unless George makes me. (He is a
right bully sometimes.)*

Have you got any brothers or sisters?

Please write soon.

Your freind Frankie

DEATHWOOD HALL

Walsea

14th Jan.

Dear Frankie,

Thank you for the drawing of Killer. He looks very fearce. I'll bet he's still alive somewhere so don't give up hope yet.

We don't live in a flat. Deathwood Hall is all ours. It has 19 rooms and a big conservatery at the back. I know it sounds big but we never seem to have enough room as there is a lot going on.

I have no brothers or sisters. I wish I had because my parents are fussy about my friends. I don't get to invite people here and I can't go out on my own so I can't visit my school friends. Victor is my best friend really (apart from you) but I also like reading. My favorite author is Helen Cresswell. Have you read *Moondial*, it's really good?

Best wishes from

Your friend Damian

13 Paradise St.
Smelby
17th Jan.

Dear Damian,

You should put your foot down about going out, its a free country. If they still wont let you, you should tell the Welfare.

What on earth do you do with 19 rooms? George was amaized. He says you could open a casino or a private loony bin or something. But if you like reading I bet youve got your own library in one of those rooms, lucky you.

I like reading. I used to go to the library down our road but I got thrown out for picking a lable off the back of a book. I didnt even know I was doing it either, because I was worrying about my history project. I got a rotten mark for it and Mr Ramsden (our teacher) was pretty mad. I think history is a waist of time. George says the only thing worth learning is how to survive.

I just came across this really funny book called *Fungus the Boggyman*. That was good, though it made me think of our cellar.

Moondial was on telly once, but I couldnt watch it because George was hoging the set.

Love from your staunch
freind

Frankie

P.S.   Im sorry to send this without a stamp but I have no money until I go to my Aunty Noras on Sunday. I know Big Brother has some (I cant think where from, he doesent get the dole) only he wont give me any. Brothers arent much use, youre better off without them.

DEATHWOOD HALL
Walsea

20th Jan.

Dear Frankie,

Fancy you telling ME to put my foot down when your brother George treats you worse than the Mafia!! Maybe you should get the Welfare to sort HIM out!

Anyway, you just don't understand the setup. We have lots of guests at our house all the time. My father brings his politicle friends home and my mother gives dinner parties for them. (So you see the 19 rooms don't get wasted. One of them is a library but most of the books are very boring.)

On party nights I have to go to bed early and watch television or read in my room, but Constance (she's our housekeeper) sometimes plays Scrabble with me or tells me about when she lived in New Zealand. She has had a very interesting and tradgick life. Her husband fell down a factory chimney and his mother had a thing called second site so she knew he was going to but nobody believed her. (They do now though.) Constance is not very good at Scrabble, she can't spell.

I have put *Fungus the Boggyman* on my Christmas list so it had better be good.

> Best wishes,
> Your friend Damian

13 Paradise St.
Smelby
24th Jan.

Dear Damian,

There was no need to be rude about my brother, but I'll forgive you because I feel sorry for you. I think its rotton that they make you go to bed while they have their dinner parties. You should go down in your pyjamas and shame them, I would. By the way, when you said all that about polotics it sudenly struck George that your dad must be Sir Edmund Drake. Fancy that - hes really famous, even I've heard of him! You arent related to Sir Francis Drake as well, are you? (Thats one bit of history I do rember.)

Do they let Victor sleep in your room? Killer used to sleep on the end of Georges bed. Sometimes George took Killer out for a walk in the middle of the night. I reckon he has insomnea. (George I mean, not Killer!) That was how Killer got lost, but George gets mad if I mension it. I exspect it makes him feel a bit stupid for losing sight of a big dog like that.

Fancy having a Christmas list! What else have you put on it?

> *Love from your interested freind*

> *Frankie*

P.S.   Have you any Enid Blyton in your library?

DEATHWOOD HALL
Walsea

28th Jan.

Dear Frankie,

Don't waste your time feeling sorry for me, I'm quite happy thank you. There's lots to do here really and it's good fun spying on the parties, you'd be surprised what they get up to!!

I don't think my family is related to Sir Francis Drake, as my father doesn't even play bowls. But my Uncle Gordon has been to two royal weddings.

Victor has a kennel next to the stables. He is not aloud into the house, except for the conservatery and

the games room, though sometimes
Constance lets him into the kitchen.
She spoils him a bit. (She's very
soft-hearted and even gives the postman tea and scones every morning.) I
have put a telly-scope on my Christmas list, as I want to be an astronom-
er. Also a word-proscesser so I can
write up my notes. Constance says at
Christmas she will give me lots of
fancy notepaper for my secret cores-
pondance - (she means for you!). She
gives my letters straight to the postman so I won't have to explain why
I'm writing to a girl as my parents are
very strict. (Maybe that's why the
postman gets the tea and scones every
morning though I think she's sweet on
him anyway, yuck!) Constance also

sorts out everybody's post in the
mornings, so she sneaks your letters
away before anyone else ever sees
them.

Do you have any secrets? I know I'm
not one, because your brother George
seems to know all about me. I hope
you don't let him read my letters.
They are PRIVATE.

Best wishes from your
friend

Damian

P.S.   I can't find any Enid Blyton in
our library. Sorry!

13 Paradise St.
Smelby
31st Jan.

Dear Damian,

I like secrets but I dont get much chance of any because of George always poking his nose in. He did find your letters, but I have now got a realy good hiding place - I hope!

Why dont you and I have a REAL secret, that would show him!! Never mind just writing, we could meet some night when your folks are having one of their boring dinner parties. Maybe we could take your Victor for a walk. I could get the bus to Walsea. It only takes half an hour from here. Then I could walk over to your place if you draw me a map. Or you could sneek out and meet me at the bus station.

Georges freind Dexter has just past his driving test. George says they are going to borow a car and have a nice day out next Saturday. So that might be a good time for our secret meeting while George is out of the way. My dad always goes to the pub on Saturday nights and comes home legless.

Let me know what you think. And do the map nice and big so I can follow it.

Your secret freind,
Frankie

P.S.   If you have no Enid Blyton what about Rodal Dahl?

P.P.S.   I wish you would learn how to spell freind.

DEATHWOOD HALL
Walsea

3rd Feb.

Dear Frankie,

You're the one who can't spell
friend only I was too polight to say so.

I like your idea of a secret meeting,
it's a brainwaive!! I'm begining to
think you're as interesting as Constance's family, but if we're going to
have secrets I hope YOUR mother
hasn't got second site!

Next Saturday would be a good time
to meet as there will be twenty guests
for dinner at our house and nobody
will have time to keep an eye on me,
not even Constance. But all the same

it will not be easy. Anybody could be looking through a window or something just at the wrong time. You must not come here or we will both be in trouble. I will try to meet you at Walsea bus station. But if I don't turn up you will know something has gone wrong and I can't get away. You won't have to be cross.

Let me know the time of the bus. I can lend you the bus fare if you are still hard up.

Your partner in crime,
Damian

P.S. Don't worry about not putting stamps on your letters. I told you Constance was sweet on the postman so he let us off.

13 Paradise St.
Smelby
7th Feb.

Dear Damian,

Now I know about the postman I
wont waist any more money on
stamps.

Dont worry about second sight (Ha!
you got that wrong!) as I havent even
got a mother now. When my dad lost
his job she went off with Mr Dowson
from the fish shop.

The bus gets in at a quarter to seven.
I will wait until half past and then get
the next bus back if you havent showed
up. I have borowed 80p from my freind
Sandra in the desk behind me, but I
will have to give it back on Monday.

As you dont know what I look like I will carry a rolled-up Beano in my left hand and I'll be eating a roar carrot. They are good for your teeth and seeing in the dark. Also they fill you up and are easy to nick off the barows.

This will be the greatest adventure of my life so far. I have never met a real hero before so dont let me down.

Yours in great antiscipation,
Frankie

P.S.   Just becase you go to St. Aidans doesent mean you can spell better than me.

Batch the Second

13 Paradise St.
Smelby
11th Feb.

Dear Damian,

*It was great to meet you last Satur-
day and I thought it was worth 80p
even though you could only stay out half
an hour.*

*Thanks for lending me the 80p to
pay Sandra back. A pity you couldnt
bring Victor, but theres always a next
time as the burgler said to the Wool-
worths ring.*

*You looked fatter than that photo in
the paper, not that I mind. I expect its
all those politicle leftovers, I should be
so lucky!*

I was home before George on Satur-

day so he didnt find out. It was after midnight when he got home. He had to thumb lifts all the way back from Blackpool as Dexter got arested. Dex borowed a car for the day, but he forgot to tell the man he borowed it from. Luckly George had just gone off for some chips when Dex got arested. You shouldve heard him telling the tale, he didnt half curse!

I hope you didnt get into trouble. Lets fix another meeting soon.

> *Your secret freind,*
> *Frankie*

DEATHWOOD HALL
Walsea

13th Feb.

Dear Frankie,

Constance saw me sneaking back in last Saturday, but she didn't tell. She says it's a shame I don't get to invite my friends in and what can they expect? I think she is our alley. So we could fix another meeting if you like.

George was lucky not to get arrested. Did he eat both lots of chips? His friend Dexter must be very forgetful. Will he have to go to prison?

Thank you for lending me your Beano. I am not aloud comics but I will keep it inside a vest in my drawer.

You were taller than I expected but I won't let it bother me.

Yours loyally,
Damian

13 Paradise St.
Stinkby
17th Feb.

Dear Damian,

Thanks for the Valentine, you should have put it in with your letter and saved a stamp as I wouldve known it was from you anyway, it mustve cost a bomb.

George reckons Dex will be put on prabation. Dex must have a terrible memory as it turns out he has done this before. Anyway, he wont do it again as he is now going to buy a car of his own. George says they will be able to go out every night, so thats a releif!

I will bring some more Beanos when

I come, so get them to nit you some more vests! What about a fortnight on Saturday for our next rondyvous if Dex has got his car by then?

You never said if you had any Rolad Dahl.

> *Your livelong freind,*
> *Frankie*

DEATHWOOD HALL

Walsea

20th Feb.

Dear Frankie,

What Valentine, I never sent you one, I thought you'd think they were yuck!

A fortnight on Saturday will be fine, as the Prime Minister is coming to dinner that night. Same time, same place? This time I will really try to bring Victor. We can go for a walk along the cliffs.

Constance had a letter from her mother-in-lore in New Zealand yesterday. She told Constance to beware as some terrible disaster was going to happen at her place of work

(that's our house)!! Constance was
very upset. I expect all it will be is a
broken dish or something. But Constance is very superstisious since her
husband fell down the chimney, I
don't blame her. I heard her telling
this to her sweetie the postman, she
practicly cried on his shoulder, yuck!
(You should have seen the Valentine
HE brought HER, in a great big
cardboard box, it was vile!)

I have just had some rotten news.
We are going to the Bahamas for a
holiday at Easter. It's the absolute
dregs. I'll have nobody to knock
around with, I hate beaches and I
detest being roasting hot all the time,
it brings me out in a rash. I will send
you some postcards but I will put

them in envelopes so George can't
read them. Did he find your new
hiding place?

No, we have no Ronald Dahl either.
Sorry!

Look forward to seeing you again.

Your great friend,

Damian

13 Paradise St.
Stenchby
24th Feb.

Dear Damian,

Well then, if you didnt send me that Valentine I must have another admierer!!! As a matter of fact I got more than one.

You shouldnt gripe about your holidays. Some of us have to make do with a run round the park. (Not that I'm jealose, I've heard the Bahamas are pretty smelly and everybody wears these daft long shorts.)

Dexter has bought his car. Well, he calls it a car, you should see it! It looks like a walking scrapyard. George says so what as long as it gets you there.

They are planning some late night excurshons. I saw a pile of sacks under Georges bed and he said they are going to get some stones to build Dex a garage. I would of thought it was better to get the stones in the daylight but those two are daft enuogh for anything.

My dad has gone off to Birmingham to look for work and is stopping there for a bit with his freind Charlie (yipee!). So that Saturday will be great, same time, same place. I'll bring some scraps for Victor.

My Aunty Nora says I can take a freind round there for tea one day, so why dont you come? She is very nice and not a bit nosey. Youd get on with her great, everybody does.

Fancy not having any Raldo Dahl, what a library!

Stay out a bit longer this time.

I'd rather have a present than post-cards (even a smelly one).

Love from your freind
Frankie

DEATHWOOD HALL

Walsea

27th Feb.

Dear Frankie,

I'm writing this sitting on the fountain steps in the rose garden. You can't get into our house for workmen. What a fuss, just because the Prime Minister is coming to dinner! We have had a new loo put in downstairs and the dining-room hall and drawing room are being redecorated. Alex - (my father's chuffeur) - has had to fetch some of our best silver from the bank. As well as all the VIPs there will be two of the P.M.'s private detectives here as well and Constance will have to see they are fed in the kitchen. Mrs Harris, our cook, is having kittens and we are hiring 2 extra girls to wait at table. I'm glad I shall be out of it.

Constance says Victor is supposed to be a guard dog - big joke! - so I don't think I'll be able to bring him after all.

If it is raining we could go to the bus station Snack Bar. I will bring some money.

Constance has got all nervous because of her mother-in-lore's letter. She keeps dropping things - (didn't I tell you she'd break a dish?) She told the postman she thinks the Prime Minister will get poisaned at our house or jam the lock in the new loo, or fall down the stairs or something, as her mother-in-lore's profesies always come true. He told her it was a load of nonsense and she said Oh Cyril you are such a comfort, yuck! But he looked very thoughtful all the same, I bet he believes it just as much as she does, what a wimp!

I won't be able to go to your Auntie Nora's but please thank her for asking me. It is too far away and I am expected to be in for tea every day. Anyway Alex (my father's chuffeur) picks me up at school so you can see it isn't easy.

I think I have a boil coming on my neck but it won't stop me meeting you.

> Greetings from your friend
> Damian

13 Paradise St.
Pongby
2nd Mar.

Dear Damian,

I am beginning to think you are a bit
stuck up. George said you would be. I
dont see why I should do all the
running about. After next Saturday
I'll have been twice to see you. So then
its your turn to come here. Cant you
make up a good tale? Like being kept
in at school or joining the Chess Club
or something? Use your imagenation -
fairs fair. In fact, if you cant promise to
come to my Aunty Noras I dont know
wether I can make it next Saturday
after all. 80p is a lot of money beside
the risk of being found out. Anyway,

what about Womens Lib?

Dex and George brought so many stones home last night they bashed a hole in the bottom of the boot, talk about laugh! The way they are carrying on, that garage is going to be as big as St. Pauls. They had so much stuff they had to get this bloke to help them. Megsy they called him, which sounds a bit sissy to me, I didnt like the look of him.

You can get special boil plasters from the cemists. They will draw it up to a head and it will burst.

I have started a Christmas list myself now just for the hell of it, it wont make any difference.

Your freind (but only just),
Frankie

P.S.   I mean what I say. Frankie the Frank, thats me!

DEATHWOOD HALL

Walsea

5th Mar.

Dear Frankie,

All right, I will try to get to your Auntie Nora's. We will talk about it next Saturday and think up a good excuse. I am not stuck up, just careful as you would be if you had parents like mine who are always thinking you'll get kidnaped, and the Prime Minister coming to dinner and stuff like that.

Please do not let me down next Saturday as I am looking forward to it very much. Meeting you is a better adventure than rescuing Victor or snooping on the VIPs or going to the rotten Bahamas three times over.

My boil is huge. Constance put me a poultise on it, it didn't half hurt. Cyril - (her boyfriend the postman, some boy!) - said I must be run down. Then he laughed and said but not by a car, eh? He thinks he is a witty comedien, groan groan, and is always trying to make friends with me this way.

Yours desperately,
Damian

P.S.   We won 4-1 last Wed. against Beckworth High, but I'm too stuck-up to tell you who saved no less than 5 goals.

13 Paradise St.
Odorby
8th Mar.

Dear Damian,

O.K. I forgive you, I am very soft-hearted actually but you have to stand up to people sometimes or they walk all over you.

So now I am all ready for Saturday - not long to go! I'm not worried about George as him and Dex have been out till all hours every night this week. They come thumping upstairs at 3 in the morning, no wonder I fall asleep in class!! Georges room is now crammed with bulging sacks. He wont let me in his room but I peeped through his keyhole just before he stuffed a bit of

rag in it. Dex should soon have his
own bus deppo never mind a garage,
always suposing they know how to
build it. I bet they dont. This Megsy
carachter is always hanging about at
nights as well now, hes the one who
finds them all the sacks.

I had a big shock yesterday, Dex got
drunk and he told me Killer was seen
off in a dog fight! Dex and George lost
a lot of money as they had backed
Killer to win. Can you believe it? I
realy loved that dog and I think Dex
and George are rotton pigs. But dont
worry I will get my own back one day!

Lets go to the Snack Bar wether it
rains or not. I'll be hungry after half
an hour on the bus and I'll need
cheering up as well. Dont forget to

bring some money.

I hope your boil is getting better. I once had one in an unmensionable place, it was agony. Dont take any notice of that daft postman, my dads freind Charlie is the same, always joking fit to make you puke. But you should pretend to laugh at his jokes though so he will go on letting us off the stamps.

> Your forgiving freind,
> Frankie

Batch
the Third

DEATHWOOD HALL

Walsea

12th Mar.

Dear Frankie,

Thank you for coming on Saturday. I really enjoyed it even with my boil and you being upset about Killer and all. I am very sorry about Killer and think Dex is the direst dregs for telling you. My thoughts about the dog fight are unmenstionable.

Nobody missed me on Saturday, not even Constance, what with all the alarm and dispondency. The Prime Minister didn't get poisaned or any- thing, but all our best silver got stolen during the night and my mother's jewels as well. Somebody came with a pile of sacks and took the lot. They left one empty sack behind, it might be a clue. Victor slept right through it, we think he was drugged.

Constance is sure this was the terrible disaster in her mother-in-lore's letter but her nerves have not improved. You would think that when the disaster was over she would calm down a bit. It doesn't seem much like a disaster to me anyway as it always takes two of them a whole day to clean that silver.

On Sunday morning Constance noticed the mud on my shoes and gave me a funny look. Maybe she thinks I pinched the silver and berried it in the garden! She wouldn't let on, though, even if I had. I heard her telling Soppy Cyril (the postman) she was more like a mother to me than my mother, (that's what SHE thinks!) Cyril said he'd noticed how close we were and good would be sure to come of it some day, what does he think he means by that?? I think he has got far too familiar lately and is always poking his nose in. You would think our kitchen was his second home.

I am glad we managed to fix up about me having tea at your Auntie Nora's. The play rehersal was a great idea for an excuse and one we can use again. If they get too interested at home I can always say the play fell through in the end because people wouldn't learn their lines.

I seem to be turning into a very

good liar! At this rate I'll be able to
follow my father's footsteps into Parliament.

> Yours truthfuly,
> Damian

13 Paradise St.
Snifby
15th Mar.

Dear Damian,

Saturday was great. I've never eaten five Chelsy buns at once before, espesialy washed down with three rasberry milk shakes.

Thank you for cheering me up about Killer. I will never get over it, though. I was so mad at George I told him if he didnt get me another dog I'd split on him about the dog-fights. They are illeagle. But I might have known - he shoved me in the cellar until I promised not to, and then he made me tell him all the latest about us. So now he knows youre going to my Aunty Noras

for tea, much good may it do him.
She's never asked HIM to tea since he
took the fiver out of her purse when he
was little.

By the way I was thinking, I'd better
meet you at your school gate as you
might not be able to find my Aunty
Noras flat on your own. That counsel
estate rambles on worse than our
Headmaster. I can easy duck out of
school for the afternoon so I'll be there
on time. You will like my Aunty Nora,
she is always good for a laugh. I
showed her the newspaper bit about
you in the well so she already thinks
you are the bees knees.

George and Dex are doing a lot of
whispering in corners these days with
their new pal Megsy. I think they are

up to something but as long as it keeps
them out of our way good luck to them.

Silver stuff always seems a waist of
money to me, think what else you could
buy!

Hows your boil?

Love from your greatful
freind
Frankie

DEATHWOOD HALL

~~Walsea~~
Walocean

19th Mar.

Dear Frankie,

Your George is a rotten bully, I don't care if he is your brother. My father is trying to put a Bill through Parliament to get stiffer sentences for thugs like him. I wish him luck. (My dad I mean, not George!) I bet they pinched those stones from a building site (and I HAVE spelt that right!). Maybe Megsy is a builder's night watchman?

Better not meet me at the school gate, somebody might see you. Wait round the corner outside the jeweler's. I'll get away as fast as I can.

Constance has had another scary letter from her mother-in-lore. She says an even worse disaster is about to befall us and this time it's something to do with me, I ask you! She must be bonkers. Soppy Cyril said she was, but Constance got mad at him so he apologised. He is so smitten with Constance that maybe he will now fix a disaster just to get back in her good books!!

Everyone believed me about the play, but Alex (my father's chuffeur) will be there to meet me with the car at six, which is when I said the rehersal would finish. So I will have to be back at the school gates for five to six at the latest, no messing. Better warn your Auntie Nora.

My boil has burst. Ugh!

Love from your enterprising friend
Damian

13 Paradise St.
Phewby
21st Mar.

Dear Damian,

Guess what, George has started asking all sorts of misterious questions about you, like what colour your hair is and how much you weigh and stuff. I think he has a cheek! He says your dad is a millionare, I dont know where he got that daft idea from unless this Megsy nutcase said it.

Maybe hes worried about your weight because Dex has offered to give us a lift to my Aunty Noras in his car - (wonders never cease!) - but I told him we'd rather walk. Its a right heap of junk and anyway we don't want him *hanging around.*

My Aunty Nora won £50 at Bingo last night, so I think we'll get a good tea, shes very genrous when shes in funds. Do you like black pudding?

Love from Frankie

DEATHWOOD HALL

~~*Walsea*~~
Wallake

24th Mar

Dear Frankie,

   I hope you refused to answer George's questions about me. He is too nosy by half. Nearly as bad as Soppy Cyril, in fact, who has taken a big interest in what I do at school break-time, as if it's any of his bisness! Constance says he is just being friend-ly but sometimes he gives me the creeps, I don't know what she sees in him.

   I have never had black pudding but I like treacle pudding. Is it nearly the same? We don't have pudding at tea-time, only useless little sandwiches and tiny bits of fruit cake, no good when you come in starving from school.

My dad is a millionaire but he hasn't got a yatch or anything like that. I know he looks really scruffy sometimes and he is always moaning about the house needing repairs. Also he is very upset about the silver, he can't think how anybody found out we had it out of the bank. Groanups never know when they are well off.

Today my mother asked me the title of the play I'm supposed to be in and all I could think of was Macbeth. She laughed and said it was bad luck to say the title of that play, you have to call it The Scotish Play as all theatre people know, and she thought the teachers would have told us. I would have to pick one like that! She asked what part I was playing so I had to say Macbeth as I couldn't remember any other carachters names. She looked very pleased and said I should make sure she had some tickets. If you ask me we are getting in pretty deep with this visit to your Auntie Nora.

I have just realised why your dog was called Killer!

> Love from your worried
> friend,
> Damian

13 Paradise St.
Whiffby
27th Mar.

Dear Damian,

Dont faint when I tell you black
puddings are made from blood, buck-
ets of it. They are very tasty. If you dont
fancy them I expect we could have tripe
and oniuns as long as we let my Aunty
Nora know in good time.

You shouldnt have picked on Macbeth, your mum will think you are a
star. You could have chose a musical
and said you were in the chorus.

George is trying to soften me up for
some reason. He has given me a broch
which he says is rubies and diamonds.
I'll bet its glass but I must say it looks

O.K. I'll wear it when we go to my Aunty Noras, then you can see it. George says if its raining that day and you get your school uniform wet your folks will know you have been out of school. So he reckons we should take the lift in Dexs car. He says its very kind of Dex to offer and he will be offendid if we dont go with him. I suppose hes got something there, if Dex gets offendid its no laughing matter, what do you think?

> Your freind for all time,
> Frankie

Batch
the Fourth

13 Paradise St,
Smelby

30th Mar.

Dear Aunty Nora,

As you have forbid me to come to your
flat I am haveing to right to you.

Our Frankie tells me you have ast her
and her boy feind to tea on the 4th. Well
I am in chardge of Frankie while our dad
is away and I dont think it is a good
idear. Dad wood be proper mad if he fond
out. She is a bit young for boy feinds I
think you will agree. So they won't be
turning up after all, but don't say nu-
thing, leest said soonest mended.

I hope your back is not playing you up
at pressent.

Your loving nepew,
George

P.S.   Burn this leter in case Frankie
ever sees it, you know how she carris on.

DEATHWOOD HALL

Walsea

30th March

Dr Ivan Fox, M.A., LL.D.,
Headmaster, St. Aidan's Academy

Dear Dr Fox,

I was delighted to hear that my son Damian had been chosen to play the part of Macbeth in your latest school production. This is just the sort of activity which will give the boy some much-needed confidence, and we at home are keen to assist in any way we can.

As a work of this calibre is bound to incur considerable expense in the way of scenery, costumes, lighting, etc., my husband and I would be glad if you would permit us to make a small contribution to the play's success (cheque enclosed).

We look forward with great pleasure to the opening night and would prefer seats in the centre of the front row if at all possible.

Yours sincerely,
Amanda Drake

DEATHWOOD HALL

~~Walsea~~
Walpond

31st Mar.

Dear Frankie,

What am I supposed to call your Auntie Nora? She isn't my auntie after all.

I think I would prefer the tripe and onions, or maybe just the onions without the tripe.

If you think we should have a lift from Dexter then O.K. It might be a bit of a laugh if we could sabotage inside the car when he's not looking, slit the seats or something, serve him right! And at least it would get us there without being seen by any bisybodies. But your George had better

not be in the car or I will not answer
for the consequences.

   Roll on the Great Day!

         Love from your stout
         difender,
              Damian

13 Paradise St.
Skunkby
2nd Apr

Dear Damian,

    Dexs car seats are already in tatters
so dont bother to bring your knife. And
dont worry, George says him and
Megsy are going to the pictures on the
Big Day so he wont bother us. He has
told me about the pictures FOUR
TIMES so he realy must be going. He
isnt a picture fan and he never tells me
what hes doing usually, I dont know
whats come over him lately.

    Call my Aunty Nora Aunty Nora,
she wont mind. Everybody does, even
the Rent Arreers.

    You cant just have oniuns on their

own, she'll think you dont like her cooking.

I tried to get a look in Georges sacks but nothing doing. He has taken to locking his bedroom door which he never use to. One sack fell over last night though and it didnt sound like stones to me. More of a clang than a crash, if you see what I mean. I am getting very suspisious in my old age!

See you Friday - whoopee!

Take care till then,

Love from Frankie

                                 13 Paradise St
                                 Smelby

                                 2nd Apr.
Dear Dex,
    We shud not be seen too gether nor
anywear near Megsy before the Big Day,
so hear is your list of instruckions.
Remember what I said - lern and burn.
    Megsy as done the ransome letter and
it is all redy to drop in the box. Bifore
you now it youll be driving a Roller
insted of that old banger.
    Dont forget to fill her up.
            Good luck and keep cool.
                                 George

Chemistry lab.
St. Aidan's Academy
4th Apr.

Dear Frankie,

I hope this letter reaches you in time. I have given it to a boy in our form who goes home to lunch and has a cousin at your school (Karen Wilkinson).

I am very sorry I will not be able to meet you today as planned but the Headmaster rang my mother up last night, and she is coming to see him this afternoon, goodness knows what for. It can't be the play as nobody at school knows about that. Anyway I will have to be here. Please give my apologies and kindest regards to your Auntie Nora. I hope you enjoy the

tripe and onions.
   In haste,
         Your bitterly disapointed
         friend,
         Damian

4, Seymour Court,
Smelby.

4th April

Dear Mr Ramsden,
   I will drop this note in on my way to work.
Please excuse Karen's absence today as she
has a very bad cold.
                    Yours sincerely,

               Lorna Wilkinson

DEATHWOOD HALL

Walsea

10 a.m., 4th April

Dear Mother-in-Law,

I do wish you would stop pestering me with all these letters of doom and gloom. As for ringing me up as you did last night, words fail me!

It has taken me long enough, but at last I have come to my senses and realised that there is nothing at all in your supposed gift of second sight. Granted, you sometimes appear to be right, but our very knowledgeable postman - (he is studying for a degree in psychology at the Open University in his spare time) - tells me that is just coincidence. What about all the times you are wrong? All that fuss on the phone last night, for instance, about an impending disaster connected with a child at my place of work was totally ridiculous. Damian is a strong, healthy boy (though admittedly prone to boils) and the worst disaster we have had here this week is burnt toast.

I am thoroughly fed up of being thrown into regular states of panic all for nothing. Why don't you take up Bridge or something for a change?

Your exasperated daughter-in-law,

Constance

P.S. I may as well tell you I won't be your daughter-in-law for much longer, as I am getting married again whilst the family is away in the Bahamas at Easter. The bridegroom will be our postman, Mr Cyril Meggs, who is very clever as I already told you, and a perfect gentleman which is more than you can say for some. Mr Meggs is about to come into some money so we are going to the south of Spain for our honeymoon.

Dr Ivan Fox, M.A. LL.D.,
Headmaster,
St. Aidan's Academy,
Walsea.

4th Apr.

To the Chairperson,
Board of Governors,
St. Aidan's Academy,
Walsea.

Dear Sir Arnold,

I write to confirm and enlarge upon our telephone conversation concerning the shocking events of today.

During the midday luncheon break, one of our pupils, Damian Drake - (whose father, as you will doubtless be aware, is none other than Sir Edmund Drake of Deathwood Hall) - disappeared from the school playground and has not been seen since. The boy's absence was not noticed until the beginning of afternoon school, at which time his mother called to see me about some strange mix-up concerning the school play.

Naturally, Lady Drake was extremely distressed when the boy could not be found, and we contacted the police immediately. In the ensuing investigation, led by Detective Superintendent Harry Hitchen, it emerged that the only outsider seen on our premises that lunchtime was our regular postman, Cyril Meggs, who had just completed the lunch-time delivery of mail. We have known Mr Meggs - (a man of impeccable character and a keen student of the Open University) - for many years, so naturally he was swiftly eliminated from our enquiries. It further emerged that Damian had lately been meeting a young lady in secret and as this seemed a much more fruitful line of approach Detective Superintendent Hitchen is presently trying to establish this young lady's name and whereabouts.

I have the gravest suspicion - (based upon my wide experience of human nature) - that there is more to this affair than meets the eye. But whether the boy is a runaway or a kidnap victim - (or even worse than that!) - I fear the adverse publicity will do the school no good at all.

Intensive enquiries are continuing and I suggest we hold a governors' meeting as soon as possible to discuss the matter further.

Yours sincerely,
Ivan Fox

13 Paradise Street,
Smelby

5th April

Dear Dad,

*I would of rung you only your freind
Charlie does not seem to be on the
phone.*

*I am writing to ask if you will come
home as soon as poss because our
George is going to be in big trouble. He
gave me a ruby and diamond broch
and I popped in to the jewelers with it
while I was having to hang about
waiting for a freind who never turned
up yesterday. I wanted to find out if the
stones were real. It turned out George
had nicked it with a lot of other stuff. I*

dont know where George is at the moment but the police have been and his bedroom door is hanging off its hinges. They have taken a lot of sacks away.

Your loving daughter,
Frances

P.S.   Aunty Nora says to tell you your chickens have come home to roast but they must be at her place, they arent here.

Passenger Lounge,
Heathrow Airport.

6th April

Sir Edmund and Lady Drake,
Deathwood Hall,
Walsea.

Dear Sir and Madam,
By the time you read this I will be halfway
to New Zealand to stay with my mother-in-
law. I shall not be coming back, and hope you
will kindly forgive the lack of notice.

I have always been very happy in your
employ and would have liked to remain with
you for many more years, but unforeseen
circumstances have caused a sudden change
in my plans. I regret any inconvenience this
may cause you.

Please give my fondest regards to Master
Damian. I hope he is now completely recover-
ed from his kidnap ordeal. If not, a good
rest and change of scene in the Bahamas this
Easter should do the trick.

I also hope that wicked, evil, deceitful,
two-faced postman Cyril Meggs gets 20 years

and serve him right.

> *Your obedient ex-servant,*
> *Constance Fisher*

P.S. If a parcel arrives for me from a shop called 'Bride Boutique' please return it at once without opening as it is just a mistake, nothing to do with me at all.

Flat 215,
Bogworth Towers,
Wildflower Estate,
Smelby (my Aunty Noras)

12th April

Dear Damian,
  I hope you like this Get Well card,
they didnt have one that said 'glad you
got saved from the kidnaper'.
  I was suprised it was Soppy Cyril
who got you, I didnt think he had it in
him. Postmen are usually drippy -
scared of dogs and trapping their
fingers in letter boxes and stuff. It just
goes to show! Now, if it had been
George and Dex, I couldve understood
it. If only theyd shaped themselves they
couldve grabbed you on the way to

Aunty Noras - IF youd turned up, I waited over an hour! - only they were too thick to think of it.

Well, youre not the only one in the papers now, what with George and Dex pinching your silver and your mums jewels and stuff to name but a few - (I told you I'd get my own back didnt I?) - and then my dad and his freind Charlie making the front page when they robbed that Bilding Society in Brum. I'm living at my Aunty Noras for good now, but she says she'll take me to court when their cases come up, it will be a lesson to me (she hopes!).

My Aunty Nora says I've never to see you nor write to you again, so I'm sending this with a girl called Karen

Wilkinson who sits near me and has a cousin at your school. Send your reply the same way.

Be seeing you!

Your freind as ever,
Frankie

DEATHWOOD HALL

Walsea

15th Apr.

Dear Frankie,

Don't tell me it hasn't dawned on you by now that your Megsy was our postman Soppy Cyril MEGGS!! (Well, it took me long enough to realise.) You know how he met George and Dex? He was here that night bringing Constance a box of chocs when they were casing the joint ready to pinch our silver. They were really chuffed that he was so well in with Constance.

Thanks for the super Get Well card even though I wasn't ill. In fact I must say I quite enjoyed being kidnaped, especially the fuss afterwards. Soppy

Cyril would never have got away with it, he bungled everything as you might expect. He grabbed me in the school playground at lunchtime and said Constance wanted me home urgently as something was up, he wouldn't say what. He had this crummy old car waiting and once he'd got me into it he gave an evil chuckle and said we were going to this empty farm a hundred miles away where nobody would ever find me. He told me him and Constance would live happily ever after abroad on the money from the randsome as he had decided to double cross George and Dex. That's why he came for me at dinner time instead of waiting till four o'clock. But I knew Constance would be mad when she found out. He hadn't told her about the kidnap, only that they would be married when he came into some money next month. Well of course chugging up this moorland road, his crummy old car broke down, didn't it - I guess it's a worse wreck than Dex's - and started sliding back. He was so busy trying to stop it I manadged to jump clear - (and a good thing too, as the car shot into a sheep fold and turned over). Soppy Cyril is now Stompy Cyril, or if you like Megsy is Pegsy, with a broken ankle, broken arm and broken heart, (always supposing he's got one!)

Me, I rolled into a peat bog, you should've seen my school uniform! I was hours staggering around trying to get help by which time I was in an even worse mess and lost a fifty quid shoe. I thought my parents would go hairless but they never said a word, only hugged me fit to bust! I was amazed as they are not the hugging sort, and what with me being so smelly and wet . . . !

Mind you, it isn't all roses, because now I am stuck at home even more than ever and we will have to be pretty cunning to fix our next meeting. A pity we have lost our alley Constance, who has suddenly taken off for New Zealand, surprise, surprise! But I will work on this new au pair Francine, she seems a good sort, very ooh-la-la! though she's utterly hopeless at Scrabble. How about the

bus station again a week on
Saturday?

> Your never-say-die hero,
>> Damian

P.S. Three cheers — the Bahamas are
cancelled!

24A Buckingham Buildings

Thrumpton.

15th April

Dear Damian Drake,

I hope you don't mind me writing to you, but I saw your photo in the paper when you were rescude from that horable kidnaper. (Fancy him being a postman, it makes you think!)

I have never writen to a famose person before. My brother Steve bets you wont write back to me but I told him you would so dont let me down.

All the best from

Tracey Fallows